THE FLAME

&

RUMINATIONS

THE FLAME

&

RUMINATIONS

THOMAS MORISON

EDITION ZORZAL

MONTRÉAL, QUÉBEC

The Flame and Ruminations

Copyright © 1998, 2012 by Thomas Morison

Library and Archives Canada Cataloguing in Publication

Morison, Thomas, author
The flame & ; Ruminations : two one-act plays / by Thomas Morison.

Issued in print and electronic formats.
ISBN 978-0-9920750-5-7 (pbk.).--ISBN 978-0-9920750-0-2 (html)

I. Title. II. Title: Ruminations.

PS8576.O6838F55 2014   C812'.54   C2014-905821-7
                                                 C2014-900077-4

Book Website www.thomasmorison.com
Editions Zorzal
Printed in Canada

THE FLAME

Characters

(Under middle age.)

HAROLD
KAROL
GISÈLE
HORN

MUSIC: Sound indications in the text are abstracted by music: meteorites, animals, are referred to in the dialogue and heard musically played on a string instrument(s). Preferably a musician or musicians are on stage.

The sound of bubbling water is to be authentic; the effect can be created by a foot operated air pump that is in the fountain.

The actors maybe ought not to be overly convinced about what they are up to, which is to say that there is a detachment in how the text might be delivered.

(A fountain. A small pool of water. Water drips occasionally from the fountain into the pool. The remains of a mausoleum, the roof has collapsed; three walls are standing. Upstage, reeds or high grass that lead back into a marsh. Backdrop of a light blue sky. Enter Harold carrying a blanket and a flashlight that is not on. He looks around. Enter Karol with a closed white umbrella and a bundle of paper. Karol and Harold look about. Harold approaches the fountain. Enter Horn. Harold nods at him. A meteorite falls, a descending glissando. They listen to it.)

HORN *(referring to music)*: Another angel dead. They should all be dead.

(Meteorite lands: glissando ends abruptly. They look into the fountain. Another meteorite falls.)

HAROLD: A seraphim?

HORN: And that for a cherub, a dead one.

(Meteorite lands.)

HAROLD: A mausoleum.

HORN: A home for some.

(Harold sets down what he is carrying. Karol leans the umbrella against the fountain.)

Stay as long as you like and watch the will-o'-the-wisps flashing, the will-o'-the-wisps; the souls of angels.

(A flash of light: a camera flash, from the marsh, a will-o'-the-wisp. Horn looks towards the light. Two more flashes.)

HAROLD: A will-o'-the-wisp.

KAROL: Ah.

> *(Karol sets down the sheets of paper next to the fountain. Harold opens the umbrella and puts it over the paper. Karol picks one sheet of paper from the stack and looks at it. Harold puts the blanket and the flashlight under the umbrella.)*

HAROLD *(pointing to the umbrella)*: I have put our things down.

KAROL: Where we can find them?

HAROLD: If we need to.

> *(Karol stares at the paper.)*

You aren't reading? *(pause)* I am going to look around. *(pause)* Until you have finished. Perhaps you will be finished by then. *(pause)* My wife.

> *(She looks up from the paper. A meteorite flies over. Crashes in the distance. Harold exits. She reads.)*

HORN: It may seem like noise at first, but after a while you hear that it is music. *(pause)* Do you like it?

KAROL: I'd have to listen to it.

> *(They listen.)*

HORN: One wants to hear almost nothing else eventually. *(pause)* After a while, one sound turns into the next, and gets louder, and LOUDER.

> *(Noise upstage of Harold approaching.)*

And then one place turns into the next.

(A flash. He exits into the reeds. Music stops. Enter Harold with a pair of crutches.)

HAROLD: Crutches.

(He hands the crutches to Karol.)

KAROL: Whose are they?

HAROLD: They were left by someone.

KAROL: Who might be looking for them, crawling around on their knees, and you've taken them.

HAROLD: Use them then if someone else can't.

KAROL: I will.

(Fountain bubbles.)

HAROLD: We can go watch the gasses burp up in the swamp.

(Fountain bubbles.)

It's full of lonely leeches.

KAROL: Lonely leeches?

HAROLD: Who only have each other to suck on.

KAROL: Only themselves.

(Harold and Karol exit. Fountain bubbles. Enter Gisèle dressed half in white and half in dark red. She has a black veil over her face. She is holding in either hand two large black handkerchiefs which trail behind her. She moves slowly to the fountain. Bends over to look into the water. Lifts up her veil. Sees her reflection. Quickly pulls down veil. Enter Horn. They are unaware of one another's presence.)

Horn looks under the umbrella. He leafs through the bundle of paper. Stops. Looks at Gisèle, she at him in the same instant. A will-o'-the-wisp flashes as they see one another. Music.)

GISÈLE: Will-o'-the-wisp.

HORN: I'm Horn.

GISÈLE: I have heard a horn.

HORN: And some sad horns will be sighing later tonight and never to be heard again.

(Music stops.)

GISÈLE: Then I have come to the right place.

(A flash. He points offstage to where he is going.)

HORN: Why not invite disaster, I ask? Though often it comes without an invitation. Though most prefer to go looking or it, and it's never very far away.

(He exits, expecting her to follow him. She looks at the small musical horns, that are on the floor downstage. She picks one up. Exits in the opposite direction as Horn. Horn re-enters looking for her. Sees that one horn is missing.)

My horns!

(Horn exits. Gisèle re-enters. She approaches the fountain. Lifts her veil. Harold enters. He is still looking around. He doesn't see Gisèle. He crosses the stage and exits. Enter Karol. Gisèle quickly lowers her veil.)

GISÈLE: Hello.

KAROL: Hello.

(*Gisèle moves away from Karol.*)

GISÈLE (*pointing to Karol's legs*): You have leeches.

KAROL: Ah.

(*Gisèle exits. Karol checks her legs. There are no leeches. Enter Harold. A meteorite is heard shooting by low overhead. They listen to it. Horn enters following the meteorite.*)

HORN: Another one, the sky is on fire.

(*Music continues.*)

That arrangement comes through the trees and over the hills, from the west and towards the east.

(*They look to the west, then east in unison. He whispers.*)

I find it is interesting to head off in that direction with one's ears perked, sneaking along with your eyes closed, in order to hear better, while walking very quietly, and listening, for the sound of disruption in the order of all things.

(*Music stops.*)

HAROLD: I will go and have a look then.

(*Harold exits. Horn goes to the fountain. Karol follows him.*)

HORN (*he gestures for her to sit*): Sit?

KAROL: Where?

HORN: Where instincts meet when the occasions arise.

(They sit on the edge of the fountain. Water bubbles from the fountain.)

HORN: An occasion is arising.

(Tempo prestissimo and passionately.)

KAROL: That doesn't happen to me.

HORN: Calling an urge.

KAROL: Calling.

HORN: Anyone who will come.

KAROL: Anyone.

HORN: I would.

KAROL: You?

HORN: If someone calls I come.

KAROL: No one but you.

HORN: But me.

KAROL: Than what --

HORN: Would be suggested instinctively.

KAROL: So quickly.

HORN: I come.

KAROL: I can be available.

HORN: Availability is important.

KAROL: I can be so available it would be almost as if I always were.

HORN: Yes.

KAROL: Oh, yes.

HORN: In the meantime. *(Tempo moderato.)* You will hear me calling.

KAROL: I'll answer. I think I will. He's coming.

(Horn exits. Enter Harold.)

HAROLD: I don't know why I left. *(pause)* Or why I came back. *(pause)* Have you seen the flies? It must be the swamp gas that attracts them.

KAROL: I am reading.

(pause)

HAROLD: There are all these flies in the water.

(He slaps the water.)

And they aren't flying.

(He violently thrashes the water. Stops.)

I couldn't find a trail that didn't end in the middle of nowhere.

KAROL: You might not have gone far enough.

HAROLD: It must be a fine thing to go away and never come back.

KAROL: Go.

(Crow call heard offstage, which is the sound of the horns when blown. Enter Horn.)

HORN: Excuse another brief intrusion.

(Harold splashes some water at Karol.)

Have you seen a horn lying about? They are black if you've seen them in the dirt, small, black.

(Horn looks in the fountain.)

HORN: You'll know what they look like if you see them.

HAROLD: If I happen to notice one.

(The men eye one another.)

HORN: It should be mentioned that one have a good look in the fountain while here, find a few wishes in the well. Wish in it. The water is a bit foggy now for some reason.

(Horn swishes the water with a hand.)

Wish, wish. Some have come from as far away as one can come, searching for a better world, while others have come in order to leave this world, only to find that there is nowhere to go, and so this has become a shrine, a monument to what can be believed, for a wish that has come true, wish, wish it would.

(Bubbles.)

There's the wish.

(Flash. Crow call offstage.)

You'll have to excuse me. I need to be here for a moment. If you could leave. If you would be kind enough to do so. That is someone coming, often no one will approach if there are others around. I am that way myself. You've been to the swamp? And in case it rains you might like to go now.

(Karol picks up the umbrella. Closes it.)

HAROLD: Possibly.

KAROL: Yes.

HORN: Nature around here has many attractions that can't be seen in one visit, or several.

KAROL: That must be true.

HAROLD: Yes.

> (*Karol prods Harold with the umbrella. Karol and Harold exit. Horn looks into the fountain. Enter Gisèle. Water bubbles.*)

HORN (*Tempo presto*): I didn't know who to expect.

GISÈLE: Neither did I.

HORN: Though when I heard the horn --

GISÈLE: You must have expected --

HORN: Then it occurred to me.

> (*He sits on the edge of the fountain, plays with the water. Meteorite passes slowly over, slow glissando.*)

GISÈLE (*moderato dolce grazioso*): There is that sense of timeless wonder.

HORN: Timeless.

GISÈLE: Wondering.

HORN: What time it is.

> (*They look into the fountain.*)

GISÈLE: Wishing.

HORN: Always for something.

> (*She sits next to him.*)

GISÈLE: Was it (*sound of meteorite stops*) dry before?

(*Bubbles.*)

HORN: Blown dry. (*pause*) Do you know from what?

GISÈLE: Innocence.

HORN: That shouldn't be a problem. Keep the horns. Blow them. I like listening to it when someone else blows my horn. Long and loud and furiously. This evening would be the best time.

(*He moves to exit.*)

Tonight by the fountain. I'll see you in the night, at the darkest hour.

(*Noises offstage. Sound of someone approaching.*)

GISÈLE: I know that hour well.

(*Flash. Gisèle exits in the direction of the flash. Horn looks at letters. Enter Harold carrying the open umbrella. He puts the umbrella over the letters.*)

HAROLD: It's about to rain at any minute.

(*It becomes suddenly dark.*)

A quick down-pour.

(*Light brightens.*)

The cloud has passed. Didn't have time to get the umbrella.

HORN: Such descriptions are useless.

HAROLD: I agree descriptions are useless.

HORN (*rhapsodizing*): From this spot the wind blows softly across the water, through the reeds and the tall grass, and around the stones and in the trees. It blows away into the distance and no one knows where it goes, the winds of change blow.

(Bubbles.)

And then there is anything that one would want to believe.

HAROLD: A miracle?

HORN: Yes, so then before history should have ended I used to be interested in the subject of miracles.

HAROLD: So was I.

HORN *(pesante)*: Then it is on account here, as a story, a piece of history, that is frequently told in this region, our local history, one particular piece of it. It is about a very old man who was one day digging a grave for his young wife and daughter, who had been killed by bandits, brutally murdered, tortured and mutilated. So horribly mutilated, that the old man had to bury his wife and daughter with his eyes closed. But unfortunately while he was digging the grave with his eyes closed he didn't notice the bandits sneaking up on him, and they robbed and killed him, too, tortured him, mutilated him. *(pause)* And I can warn you that from that time on, I have had to be careful myself. You never know who is there, lurking in the bushes with a knife between his teeth, and a spade under his arm.

(Music in the distance.)

HORN: The passions at play. And it's getting foggy.

(Owl hoots.)

HORN: That was a horned owl calling. And the wind is coming up. It will be night soon and in the dark, descriptions are even more useless.

(*Horn exits.*)

HAROLD: Karol. (*softly and gently.*) Come to me. Come love. My love. Come.

(*Enter Karol.*)

KAROL: Don't ask for me like that.

HAROLD: It is getting dark.

KAROL: Yes, it is.

(*It is slowly becoming darker. Karol picks up the blanket, the letters, and the flashlight, and goes into the mausoleum.*)

I am going to get ready to sleep.

(*Harold goes into the mausoleum. Cleans out some bones and other remains.*)

HAROLD: You are tired.

KAROL: I don't want to be awake.

(*They settle down to sleep in the mausoleum, covering themselves with the blanket. Lights dim. Night falls. Music, which is representative of animal activity. Some roaring noises perhaps.*)

My God.

HAROLD: It's not easy for animals either.

KAROL: Maybe one of us should stay up, while the other sleeps. (*pause*) You stay up, and I'll sleep, if you could be trusted.

HAROLD: No, I can't be, neither can you.

KAROL: There is no point in both of us staying up.

HAROLD: We might have to in order to make sure neither goes to sleep.

(*Man shrieks offstage. Music stops.*)

God Almighty.

KAROL: Jesus.

HAROLD: The man without his crutches.

(*They cuddle up to each other. Music.*)

KAROL: Ah well, I'll stay up.

(*It is almost completely dark. Flash offstage. Karol turns the flashlight on and off several times.*)

HAROLD: Fire flies.

(*She shines the flashlight on a letter.*)

The animals are dreaming of being human.

(*Music stops. Silence. She twirls the flashlight in the air.*)

KAROL: I am writing you from the light of a lighthouse. I don't have much time between the turns to write. It just turned, but that gives me time to think. There it goes again. I just missed a turn while thinking. You'd like it out here. There it goes again. This is frustrating, and I have so much I want to tell you. But I'll have to wait till the morning.

HAROLD: I remember that. I was thinking of you all

night.

KAROL: You'd have fallen asleep.

HAROLD: I didn't. The light kept me up.

(She shines the light in his eyes.)

KAROL: All night?

(Music. Music stops. He yawns.)

I am blowing kisses to you with every breath, and every breath I take is for you, and every heartbeat is for you. *(pause)* My love, my flesh burns, my bones melt, my brain turns to mush. All I am is what I want of you. Everything there is, reminds me of you. My moments of happiness, and when I am sad—it's because of you. *(pause)* I have no life really, none to speak of. I hope that is all right.

(Pause. She turns off the flashlight.)

I am writing you from inside of your embrace. It's warm here, and I can hear your heart beating next to mine, barely, it's hardly beating, sometimes I wonder if you are dead, but at least you are warm. There is no wind tonight, it's quiet except for the animals reminding us that we are human to the touch. You are still here with me, but so far away, lost in your thoughts, and in mine, which is better than no thoughts at all.

(pause)

HAROLD *(quietly)*: What are you thinking?

KAROL: Nothing.

HAROLD: You must be getting tired. *(pause)* I am almost

tired. *(yawns.)* It's this yawning that keeps me up.

> *(They yawn loudly together. Lights fade on them. Sound of horse hooves walking. Enter Gisèle and Horn.)*

GISÈLE: The sounds of the night.

> *(Bubbles. A meteorite rises in the sky.)*

HORN: Another shooting star.

GISÈLE *(shot by a star?)*: It got me that one!

> *(He sits down. She sits next to him.)*

HORN: This is the kind of misery I like. This is the best misery I've known in a long time.

GISÈLE: It's not unpleasant.

HORN: A longing kind of sadness that by morning will be completely hopeless.

GISÈLE: Hopeless. *(pause)* Hopelessly sad.

HORN: For a day that might never come. Longing to.

GISÈLE: Go down.

HORN: And this feeling of longing and hopelessness. We long so much and long for more and long, as the day is long.

GISÈLE: And the night, too.

HORN: Longing for the day.

> *(Bubbles.)*

HORN: When it comes. *(pause)* Oh well.

GISÈLE: Well, well.

HORN: The moment that someone has been waiting for will never come maybe.

GISÈLE *(swooning)*: Woe oh woe.

HORN: Miserable misery and contempt and some disgust and bitterness, and a little more misery with some nausea, and lots of hate and extra contempt with more disgust. A recipe for life.

GISÈLE: Those are the ingredients.

HORN: And they are poisonous, deadly poisonous, or will make us sick if nothing else. *(pause)* Could you take your veil off?

GISÈLE: It doesn't come off.

(Flash.)

HORN: Can you see anything under there? *(Flash.)* Under your veil?

GISÈLE: Only tears.

HORN: Does it come up at least?

(He lifts up her veil.)

GISÈLE: Not for long.

(She pulls it back down.)

HORN: You are beautiful, even in the dark.

GISÈLE: Especially in the dark.

HORN: You could be beautiful.

GISÈLE: I'm not. I am very ugly.

HORN: Another reason to be miserable.

GISÈLE: It's going to be a long night by the end of it.

HORN: And at the darkest hour.

GISÈLE: It hasn't come yet, almost, but not quite yet.

HORN: And why not take the time to see what the night will bring and walk out into it with me, into the darkest misery where hope is a forbidden word.

GISÈLE: I wish it were.

HORN: And it may come true. *(pause)* You'll need a place to sleep amongst the reeds.

GISÈLE: And when the darkest hour comes.

(Blackout.)

HORN *(whispering)*: Where are you?

GISÈLE *(whispering)*: It's come. And you?

(Sun comes up.)

HAROLD: It's me. Wake up. Are you up?

KAROL: You are waking me up.

HAROLD: I am trying to.

(He nudges her.)

KAROL: Go back to sleep.

HAROLD: I can't. I am awake.

KAROL: You were supposed to stay up.

(pause)

HAROLD: What if before we get up?

KAROL: I am not up.

HAROLD: Before we get up.

KAROL: What?

(*pause*)

HAROLD: I won't beg.

KAROL: I am too tired.

HAROLD: Then go back to sleep for a while.

KAROL: I'd still be too tired.

HAROLD: So would I.

KAROL: Go back to sleep and you would have something to dream about.

HAROLD: I can't remember dreams now.

KAROL: They have failed you.

(*pause*)

HAROLD: Yes, they have, like yours and everyone's, and I thought I was different. (*Some moaning offstage. Music.*)

KAROL: I hope that isn't you.

HAROLD: No.

(*Music stops. A moan.*)

KAROL: The man still isn't dead.

(*pause*)

HAROLD: He is someone else. Maybe it's me.

KAROL: Yes, it is.

(*pause*)

HAROLD: I'll go and see who.

KAROL: Go.

(Harold exits. Enter Horn.)

HORN: Good morning. Did you sleep well?

KAROL: Yes, except for the animals were loud and it was a little cold.

HORN: He's away.

(Sound of horse hooves.)

That's the black beast. And according to tradition it is said that if you can ride that horse until it dies it will take you to heaven, where he'll change colour when he gets there. So then turn white amongst the dark clouds. But I don't think anyone will ever make it.

KAROL: I suppose not.

HORN: Not even if there was the slightest chance of it happening.

KAROL: There wouldn't be much of one.

(He rubs her for warmth.)

HORN: Unless something changes with some encouragement to stay warm on the coldest days and nights.

KAROL: I shouldn't.

HORN: Proof can't be denied.

KAROL *(excited)*: Ooh, so much proof. And last night I heard the horse running, and I imagined he was running through the sky amongst the stars and in the clouds, neighing away, neighing. And I have never heard a horse neighing like that.

HORN: But you said yes.

KAROL: I imagined it.

HORN: So much depth. The bush is over here, and thick and soft, and deep.

KAROL: I'll get my umbrella.

HORN: I'd like to show you around and everything there is.

(*Horse trotting. She gets her umbrella.*)

KAROL: Yes.

HORN (*referring to the umbrella*): You'd look beautiful riding him with that, and he'd make it to heaven with you on top of him. I would.

(*Horse galloping. They go into the reeds. Enter Gisèle. She looks into the water. Lifts her veil. Enter Harold.*)

HAROLD: I thought you were my wife for a moment.

(*pause*)

GISÈLE: I am a widow.

HAROLD: Sorry.

GISÈLE: Recently widowed. You didn't notice the veil.

HAROLD: My wife was once a widow.

GISÈLE: Yes, we have met.

HAROLD: Ah, we were going to eat soon. If you would like to join us?

GISÈLE: I could, yes.

HAROLD: I felt bad, so I thought I'd invite you.

GISÈLE: Thank you.

HAROLD: It will be soon I believe.

GISÈLE: Later then.

>   (*pause*)

HAROLD: One could wait.

GISÈLE: I have some mourning to do, which I like to do at this time of the day, so I have the rest of the day to myself.

HAROLD: You mourn everyday.

GISÈLE: Yes, I must, otherwise I'd die from sadness. (*pause*) I must go.

>   (*She exits. Enter Karol.*)

HAROLD: I thought you would be waiting for me.

KAROL: I wasn't even thinking of waiting for you.

HAROLD: When did you want to eat?

>   (*He brushes some reeds off her.*)

KAROL: My umbrella blew away.

HAROLD: Again?

KAROL: You can go look for it.

>   (*Enter Horn with umbrella.*)

HORN: Miss.

KAROL: Ah.

(Horn pumps the umbrella, opening and closing it several times. Throws it up in the air. Catches it coming down.)

HORN: The clouds are falling.

(Harold takes the umbrella and closes it.)

HAROLD: What should I do with it?

(He throws it in the fountain. It sinks. Music. They listen. Crow call sounds. Flash offstage.)

HORN: Ah, nature never stops, does she?

(Music stops.)

KAROL: And lunch?

HORN: Of course.

(Horn exits.)

HAROLD: So I found some more crutches, a mound of them in a hole, in a pit and it was alive with insects and worms, crawling all over each other, millions of them and flies were crawling over the worms. It was wiggling and swarming with flies and worms, oozing in this pit, full of slime and what was it, I asked? What?

KAROL *(sincerely)*: I believe you.

HAROLD: I saw the woman with the veil. She said you had spoken with her. I invited her to eat with us. I don't think she'd eat very much a woman like that, since we don't have very much, either that, or she'd be a complete pig. *(pause)* You won't come and have a look at the pit. We could then sit down afterwards and have a good meal, talk about whatever comes to mind, and possibly we will find the man we heard.

KAROL: Why don't you get a pair of crutches of equal height? Before we eat.

HAROLD: I have nothing better to do.

(Harold exits. Enter Gisèle, carrying a letter.)

GISÈLE *(referring to letter)*: This was... in a burning bush.

(Gisèle gives a letter to Karol. Karol puts it with the other letters.)

You have so many.

KAROL: I seem to.

GISÈLE: If they were mine I'd have burnt them.

KAROL: I ought to.

GISÈLE: If you want to burn anything there is a fire.

KAROL: A flame.

GISÈLE: You have heard of it?

(Karol shrugs.)

It is the eternal flame of love.

KAROL: ?

GISÈLE: A flame of burning desire—symbolic of the eternal burning desire of love is how it's been referred to. If I can assist you, though I doubt I could be of much help.

(Karol picks up a few letters to burn.)

KAROL: A sym, sym, symbolic flame?

GISÈLE: It's always hard to say.

KAROL: Not always.

GISÈLE: Most of the time. *(pause)* Would you like a hand?

KAROL: I can manage.

GISÈLE: It should be still burning, after all, it is eternal.

> *(Karol has the letters. They exit. Enter Harold with an arm full of crutches. He drops them near the fountain. A large flame blows up in the sky behind him. Meteorite. Enter Horn. A light flash. They watch the sky.)*

HORN: A meteorite shower.

> *(Looking up.)*

Pouring.

> *(pause)*

Then you are looking for some pear-a-meters, one should be. It's dangerous to be out without one's pear-a-meters. You never know where you'll end up without your pear-a-meters.

HAROLD: Pear-a-meters? *(correcting the pronunciation of parameters)* Parameters. No, I am looking for my wife.

> *(Harold exits. Enter Gisèle. Music.)*

HORN: So passions are playing again like last night, which was a tale that was never told. Then would you like to have any expectations?

GISÈLE: I certainly would.

HORN: Assuming that some particular assumption is

worth making and so it's a matter of what to expect then.

(*They move towards each other. Tempo presto.*)

Assuming that.

GISÈLE: Yes, that.

HORN: Beyond all assumptions.

GISÈLE: That would be.

HORN: All things beyond themselves. But there are others here, who are coming. They are coming.

GISÈLE: To eat.

HORN: To eat, you say?

GISÈLE: So then on my way here I was almost hit by a meteorite.

HORN: But the chances of that happening.

GISÈLE: Are a thousand to one.

HORN: Beyond the most remote possibility.

GISÈLE: I'd be scared to think of it.

(*Music fades. Enter Karol.*)

KAROL: Hello.

HAROLD: Hello.

(*Enter Harold with more crutches. He puts them with the other crutches. The following section should progress quickly rising in intensity to Horn's: Celebrate.*)

HORN: What a gathering.

GISÈLE: There is only one thing to do.

KAROL: Food.

HORN: Eat.

HAROLD: Something to drink.

KAROL: We haven't much.

> *(From a pocket Karol pulls out a piece of paper, in which is wrapped some pickles.)*

HORN: I only have crumbs myself.

KAROL: Pickles?

> *(Karol passes the paper with the pickles in it. Each of them takes a pickle.)*

HORN: Pickles!

> *(Karol spreads the blanket for them to sit on.)*

HAROLD *(referring to the blanket)*: It's wet from the dew.

KAROL: Sit. Sit.

> *(Harold sits on the blanket.)*

HORN: It is wet.

> *(Horn throws a pickle into the fountain.)*

I have something to drink.

> *(Horn takes out a bottle.)*

We have my horns which we can drink from.

> *(He gets the horns. Horn pours out the content from the bottle into the wide end of the horns. He passes them out to all.)*

HORN: It is terrible stuff though, the foulest drink you'll have ever had, and its effect is evil—drink a little, and almost as soon as you have, instantly, in fact, you will despise everyone and everything around you, and if you drink enough, you'll hate yourself. I have seen it happen after one little sip. But, of course, I am saying this so you will try it.

> *(Tempo presto.)*

GISÈLE: A toast?

HORN: That would be a timely sentiment.

HAROLD: A toast.

GISÈLE: To us.

> *(Meteorite. The sound of the meteorite musically develops melodically and harmonically. It increases in volume. Horn sets down the bottle.)*

HORN: May your feasts be full of flavour and may the after-taste always be with you.

GISÈLE: Why not celebrate.

> *(They down the contents of their horns. Karol blows her horn. Gisèle blows her horn. Harold blows his horn. The sound is of three crow callers. They are trumpeting. It is considerable in volume. Horn moves away from them. Horn speaks screaming over the horns.)*

HORN: Celebrate. Eat well and hardy. And may all your thoughts blossom into flowers and turn to fruit to be eaten as food for thought. Celebrate! Call the animals to come out and join us. The dancing bears, and the lions and horses. Celebrate.

(Music and horn blowing stops.)

HORN: Quieter.

(Karol blows her horn once quietly. Gisèle then blows her horn once, louder. Horn blows his horn as loud as possible. Silence.)

And the silence afterwards. *(pause)* Significance is what you make of it.

(Bubbles.)

Isn't it? Significance is what you make of it.

(Bubbles.)

Or maybe not. *(pause)* Look in the water for a wish if there is one you want. I think there is one.

(Horn goes over to the fountain. Karol follows. They look into the water.)

KAROL: Yes, there is one.

HORN: At the bottom it goes as far down as the sky goes up. True exaggeration knows no limits. It's tempting enough to make you want to see to the bottom of things.

KAROL: Your wish?

HORN: We can take up where we left off before your umbrella blew away.

KAROL: I ought to refuse.

HORN: Another condition. Do you know how many conditions there are for this and that?

KAROL: Many.

HORN: Then you could be wearing a veil in memory of someone.

KAROL: Oh?

HORN: A shroud.

KAROL: How?

HORN: Riding the black beast. Follow me.

(Horn and Karol move off into the reeds. Exit.)

GISÈLE: More?

(Gisèle picks up the bottle, pours Harold some more.)

HAROLD: Thank you. *(pause)* I think he is right about its effect.

GISÈLE: It is the opposite for me.

HAROLD: I'd like to ask a personal question about myself. Do I have the appearance of someone capable of causing another person to suffer? Could I hurt the woman who loves me?

GISÈLE: No, really you may just be too sensitive.

HAROLD: Which is a terrible fault, I know.

(She lifts up her veil.)

GISÈLE: More?

HAROLD: I'll get drunk then. I am already.

(Gisèle gives him the bottle.)

HORN *(offstage)*: Another condition!

GISÈLE: That's all right. I am accustomed to drunks.

HAROLD: Was your deceased in love with you?

(She nods.)

HAROLD: He loved you?

GISÈLE: More than I thought possible. More than I wanted. I can't believe I was once loved like that. It seemed as if it would never end. Day after day, endlessly. *(pause)* He used to make love to me until I was almost blind—and ever since I have worn this veil in his memory. I have been blinded by love. *(pause)* Which is why I will mourn him for the rest of my life, until one day I will go blind. Je me suis livrée en aveugle au bonheur d'aimer. Je l'aimais. Quant je rêvais de lui, je rêvais tout haut, je criais mille fois de suite que "je t'aime". Il était un homme comme on n'en trouve plus de nos jours, avec une façon d'être. Il ne manquait pas de présence. Il était toujours là. Prêt à bondir. A vouloir faire son devoir. J'aurais tellement voulu venir ici avec lui pour voir la flamme eternelle de l'amour. Elle était si chaude la flamme. On était si bien l'un contre l'autre.

HAROLD: He loved you.

GISÈLE: I didn't have to ask.

HAROLD: No one has asked me.

GISÈLE: That's unfortunate.

HAROLD: No threat from me was what I ever hoped for.

(He throws the bottle into the fountain. The bottle breaks.)

It's finished.

(Enter Horn. Music.)

HAROLD: Your wine was poison. And where is Karol?

HORN: Lost in the bushes. I don't know where she is. Somewhere in the bushes. And won't be found. I looked for her. You may have just lost your wife.

HAROLD: I know I have. I have lost her. She is gone. I shall never see her again.

(*Playing with Gisèle's veil.*)

HORN (*to Gisèle*): He's drunk.

GISÈLE: He's sad.

HORN: Oh God, your veil is so beautiful and soft, velvety, gentle.

HAROLD (*drunk*): She enjoys herself when I am not around. Karol. You are reading my thoughts? I can feel you reading my thoughts, leafing through them, as if I were a cheap romantic novel that when you get to the end you cry because you wanted me to be the man you loved.

(*Music stops.*)

GISÈLE: That book has been burned.

HAROLD: What book?

HORN: The smoke.

(*Gisèle lifts up her veil for Horn.*)

GISÈLE: It's the flame, (*music*) an eternal flame. It flares up as red as you have ever seen and may begin to burn out of control. Wildly out of control. So there may be something to it.

HORN: If there is anything to it—

GISÈLE: It's a magnificent fire, started by a meteorite.

HORN: From some distant star.

GISÈLE: The most distant of them all.

HORN: And it's come.

GISÈLE: There.

HORN: Where?

> *(Horn and Gisèle exit. Harold rolls around on the wet blanket. Enter Karol.)*

HAROLD: You're listening to the music.

KAROL: You're drunk?

HAROLD: No, I am just unhappy, a little.

KAROL: You're drunk.

HAROLD: I am unhappy all the time now. I am completely miserable. I can't remember the last time I felt so terrible. I don't think I would even be consolable any more.

KAROL: You wouldn't be.

HAROLD: I'm not.

KAROL: Where did they go?

HAROLD: To listen to the music.

KAROL: Where?

HAROLD: To the pit.

KAROL: Something is burning.

HAROLD: A fire pit.

> *(Karol moves to exit.)*

HAROLD: Wait. I'll come with you.

> *(They exit. Enter Horn and Gisèle covered in soot. Music stops.)*

HORN: We fell right into that.

GISÈLE: Oh well.

HORN: Any other ideas?

> *(Gisèle takes a letter from a pocket. Gives it to him.)*

GISÈLE: This. Read it.

> *(He reads.)*

And there are more.

HORN: Hmm.

GISÈLE: What?

HORN: I am reading it.

GISÈLE: What do you think of it?

HORN: Indulging in this sort of thing requires a certain kind of sensibility.

GISÈLE: You have mud on your behind.

> *(She rubs the muddied soot from his face. He brushes the soot off her.)*

HORN *(reading letter with great difficulty, he can't read)*: We are so happy to be alive even at times when we'd be better off dead. You know, I am reflecting on all the things we discussed and said to each other that have made us so happy, and it doesn't seem possible to be so in love and so happy.

(Gisèle stands closer to him. They look at each other.)

HORN: Could it be? *(reads)* The more I think of you, the more I wish you thought like me, and I thought like you. If we were that close. Imagine if we were, and then we'd be who we were always meant to be— the greatest lovers who ever lived. Gods of flesh! Carnal croatians of pleasure. Carnal crustaceans of pleasure! *(correcting himself)* Carnal creations of pleasure.

(They embrace. He releases her.)

GISÈLE: Oh yes.

HORN: You read it.

(He gives her a letter.)

GISÈLE *(reads quickly)*: Charge. Charge! You are coming at me like an army of strong young men. Invade me. Ride me into the wilderness and may we never come out of it.

(pause)

HORN: Are they there?

GISÈLE: Here they come.

(Music. Horn and Gisèle separate. Gisèle drops the letter in the fountain. Karol and Harold enter covered in soot.)

HORN *(to Karol and Harold)*: You too.

KAROL and HAROLD: Yes.

HORN: Listen to that. *(pause)* One can appreciate the music, and be compelled by it. Here is what's meant, as it is supposed to sound, when it comes together, like this. We can dance around like fools to celebrate this moment. *(Horn takes a step or two.)* So this is a good time to surrender to the moment, to this very moment.

GISÈLE: Now.

HORN: Or in a millennium. Nothing will be the same, not even remotely.

(Music fades out.)

But that won't be the end of it, not in a thousand years. So you can hear it at times underground and between your ears. Then ants are dancing in their holes. Snakes are wiggling in their skins.

HAROLD: But I must be deaf.

(Bubbles. Horn gets into the fountain. Splashes about. A meteorite rises in the sky.)

HORN: One of those is going past us forever into eternity, wait, wait for us.

(Gisèle gets in the fountain with him. Lights dim. Moon comes out.)

KAROL: May I join you?

HORN: You must join me. Everyone.

(Karol gets into the fountain.)

GISÈLE: Are you coming in?

HORN: Get him in here.

(Music. Gisèle takes Harold by the hand and leads him into the fountain.)

GISÈLE: Come on. Sit down.

> (*They sit in the water, lying back, their heads emerging. Music stops.*)

KAROL: The music stopped.

HORN: It will return.

> (*Long silence.*)

KAROL: When?

HORN: Listen.

> (*Long silence.*)

HAROLD: Well, if I could sing I would.

KAROL: He wrote me notes with songs in them, but I never knew what they sounded like.

HAROLD: You probably didn't.

KAROL: Do you remember one?

HAROLD: It wouldn't be like it was then.

KAROL: I wouldn't know if it was or wasn't.

HORN: Sing for the swans.

HAROLD: I'll sing as I might have sung.

> (*He hums, warbling, croaking. Stops.*)

I forget the words.

HORN: Fuck the words!

> (*Harold croaks, screams at the top of his lungs.*)

KAROL: Sing the melody.

HAROLD: I've forgotten the melody.

HORN: Fuck the melody! Who needs melody? There are no more melodies.

HAROLD: No?

HORN: Sing for the future, it sounds good to me.

(Music.)

HAROLD: Yes, I can sing. I'll sing. I have been harbouring horrible thoughts and always have, about you and what I think about myself is even worse. I think we are lamentable, especially me, but I feel bad for you, too.

KAROL: So do I.

HAROLD: Had we known each other since we were children, perhaps we would have done all our fighting then, and it wouldn't have been so terrible for us now, but nothing but joy and things that we could remember, and would want to remember. *(Referring to the mausoleum.)* Then that house is so much like the one where I grew up with the wall missing and there never were any doors to open or any windows to look out of or anything, but a few old memories that weren't even our own. I remember being hungry. I remember lying awake at night and dreaming of the food I wouldn't be able to eat the next day. And my dreams always came true then.

(Music stops. He moves about in the water. Harold giggles. Thrashes.)

GISÈLE: What is he doing?

HAROLD: There is a tickle. Don't tickle me. Please, no, I shouldn't be laughing. You are tickling me. Stop it.

KAROL: No, I am not tickling you.

HAROLD: You are.

KAROL: I'm not.

HAROLD: Stop.

KAROL: You stop.

HAROLD: Augh. I've cut myself. I am cut. I have been cut. I'm cut. It hurts. *(pause)* That's better, yes.

 (pause)

HORN: Blood.

KAROL: The glass.

HAROLD: I am bleeding.

HORN: Don't move. It will make it worse.

GISÈLE: Does it hurt?

HORN: Don't move. No one move!

 (The water turns red. Horn picks up a pickle from the water. Gives it to Harold.)

Relax.

 (Harold eats the pickle.)

HAROLD: It doesn't hurt.

HORN: Just be glad the water is warm.

KAROL: Are you cold?

HAROLD: Suddenly I am cold now that you mention

it. So was that me screaming?

HORN: No, don't excite yourself.

HAROLD: I was a moment ago, but now, I am relaxed.

> *(Harold gets out a letter from a shirt pocket and gives it to Karol.)*

Then I am floating. And I feel an ebb flowing out of me. I wrote that to you, didn't I? You were my ebb flowing into me. Read me my last letter.

KAROL: You were going to send it, but you never did.

HAROLD: That was my last letter. Read the last paragraph.

> *(Karol unfolds the letter.)*

Read it.

KAROL: Dear Karol.

HAROLD: The last paragraph!

KAROL: My love. This is my last letter. I will miss you. But having been with you will certainly make up for that. At least I hope it will.

HAROLD *(reciting what he had written)*: Seems as if you were a different person once, so was I. I feel old and decrepit. Then for some time now in the mornings when I get out of bed I am completely ungrateful for being alive. If I have any dreams I consciously try to forget them, fortunately I have few. Nothing pleases me. There are no more pleasures. Not even food provides me pleasure. My discomfort has become my only comfort. What I am saying now, for instance, is causing an enormous amount of pain, and at this moment there is just about anything I would rather be doing, anything rather than be here bleeding, regretting my life. I'd rather do anything than die. Than be here bleeding to death in a pool of blood. *(pause)* I'd like to say something in Latin. Te amo, amas, amat, amamos. Tenebris agit. My last words from a dead language.

(Karol drops the letter in the water. Owl hoots. Horn, Karol, and Gisèle sing a Gregorian rendition of the following verse.)

Soles occidere et redire possunt:
Nobis cum semel occidit brevis lux,
Nox est pepetua una dormienda.
Da mi basia mille, deinde centum.

(Night falls. The water is dark red. Their faces emerge from the red water.)

HORN: How beautiful. We should see ourselves.

GISÈLE: Beautiful.

HORN: I would die myself for beauty.

GISÈLE: We should never have to move.

HORN: Or be moved. Freeze. And we can wait until the winter comes.

(Karol gets out of the fountain.)

KAROL: My feet are numb, my legs are numb. So I'll leave while I still can. Excuse me.

(She takes a pair of crutches of uneven height from the pile. Uses them. Exits.)

HORN: You'll stay?

GISÈLE: Will you?

HORN: I think of it as remaining.

> *(Flash.)*

GISÈLE: When I arrived I wondered if I looked as mournful as I am. And if I was as sad as I am now.

HORN: You look sad.

> *(pause)*

GISÈLE: Thank you.

HORN: It should start to fog over and rain.

GISÈLE *(she feels around in the water for the umbrella)*: If it rains.

HORN: Their umbrella.

> *(Horn brings the umbrella out of the water. It is red. He opens it.)*

GISÈLE: Close it, it's dripping.

HORN: It has started to rain.

GISÈLE: It is just dripping.

> *(They embrace. The umbrella closes around their heads.)*

HORN: Under your veil I can see a tear. You can't hide them anymore.

> *(They move under the umbrella. Animal noises in the distance.)*

GISÈLE: My hidden tears will never come, you can't see them.

HORN: As the flood waters recede they come.

GISÈLE: It would have to be the tides going out for me.

HORN: I am holding back myself.

GISÈLE: Hold on.

(*Bubbles.*)

HORN: How long?

GISÈLE: Until I have to go.

HORN: And so how can change take place if we don't let go of what there is? But then again, how is a serious question asked without it becoming ridiculous and meaningless?

GISÈLE: It doesn't matter.

(*They move under the umbrella.*)

HORN: Should we remove our clothes, strip ourselves?

GISÈLE: After what has happened.

HORN: No, of course. (*pause*) We'll just listen to the animals then for a while, maybe that will help.

(*Harold emerges from the water.*)

HAROLD: Karol? She's gone. (*pause*) I have stopped bleeding. I ought to be dead. There is no reason why I shouldn't be. Is there? She has gone, hasn't she?

GISÈLE: Yes.

HAROLD: I am going to regret having lost so much and having had so little to begin with, but even still, it hurts to lose what you never had. Then you are in my blood and I have lost a lot. So could I keep the umbrella?

GISÈLE: Certainly.

> (*Harold takes the umbrella off them. Horn has Gisèle's veil in his teeth.*)

HAROLD: We had lost this so many times and always when it rained. (*pause*) I think I'll go and live the easy life. Yeah, that's what I'll do.

> (*Harold exits twirling the umbrella. Horn takes the veil from his mouth, lets it drop into the water.*)

GISÈLE: He wasn't such a bad person.

> (*Lights dim. Horn holds out a hand to see if it is raining.*)

HORN: Now we are going to get wet.

GISÈLE: The fire must be out.

HORN: By now it would be.

GISÈLE: Love is not eternal, not even for as long as it lasts.

HORN: It should be.

GISÈLE: Why have you been in this place for so long?

HORN: Seemed like the place to be at one time.

GISÈLE: There must be another reason.

HORN: Perhaps.

> (*pause*)

GISÈLE: Were you about to leave when I came?

HORN: No.

GISÈLE: What were you doing?

HORN: Looking for someone to come.

GISÈLE: I am glad I did. I haven't felt this way since the great lose in my life.

HORN: I'll be sorry when you leave.

GISÈLE: Could it be possible to cry oneself to death?

HORN: There are easier ways.

GISÈLE: I'd prefer for it to be difficult.

(Karol enters on the crutches.)

KAROL: I have returned for my umbrella.

HORN: Someone came and got your things.

KAROL: Who?

HORN: A thief.

KAROL *(as if asleep, droning)*: A metaphor for something. Things. I didn't need them.

HORN: He took the umbrella. It looked like it was going to rain so he took it.

KAROL: I have no more feelings about my things. So I don't think I'm ever going to have any children. I'd have nothing to give them.

(Karol limps off. Gisèle gets out of the water.)

HORN: It's not often there is any reason for anyone to come here, and it may be a long time before there is any reason for anyone to do anything, and by then you and I will most certainly be dead, murdered, tortured and mutilated, according to tradition, which isn't as bad as it may seem, nothing should be. *(beat)* Be careful not to get yourself hurt or killed.

GISÈLE: I'd die of sadness before I would be killed.

HORN: Be careful.

GISÈLE: I shall.

HORN: And wish me well.

GISÈLE: I'd like to.

(*pause*)

HORN: This is the next time then, and it feels like the last.

GISÈLE: The next to the last.

HORN *(he splashes at the letters on the surface)*: What will I do with this litter?

GISÈLE: He will come back for them?

HORN: Not likely.

GISÈLE *(she points at what is a heap in the mausoleum)*: Or someone could be sent to fetch them, someone like him. *(pause)* Don't you wish this was you?

HORN: Well, I have had such thoughts.

GISÈLE: Today would be a nice day to disappear.

HORN: For some.

GISÈLE: It is so quiet, like death.

(*pause*)

HORN: And the world is relenting. The world, and someday the universe, but first the world.

(*She moves towards a wing. Stops. Remains there,*

watching him. A donkey brays in the distance. Tempo rallentendo.)

HORN: One is as one was, alone in this world, and in the universe for that matter. The stars are shining, so is the moon, there are obviously no clouds in the sky. The grass is dry and even the weeds are dying, silently swaying in the wind. The sound of crumbling bones and stones and the distant braying of a donkey is all I can hear. *(beat)* The donkey has stopped, but the bones. I can't imagine how things would be different at this moment, well yes I can. It is once again as it was a moment ago. A cloudless moonlit night. A night to look out into the dark, a mystical dark night, a miracle is almost waiting to happen. I have been forced to imagine it. The moon falls out of the sky, I don't know why. I wait for one miracle, proof of the existence of all things. One final ultimate condition met!

(Donkey brays.)

I have waited. Nothing. There's the donkey again. He sounds frustrated, donkeys usually do, and don't some of us know how he feels, working all day and no pleasure at the end of it. Of course, it is possible that the donkey is braying in ecstasy, dreaming in his donkey dreams of some pure and tender moment when His Master will be kind to him. But let us ask if it is possible, that although he is a beast of burden, could his burden be as great as ours?

(Donkey brays.)

The female donkey is braying now, the two are

braying, they are rubbing their gentle tendernesses together by the sound of it, and if I can believe it, horns from a church are being blown, ah, the horns, the donkeys, life. *(beat)* But at least someone, somewhere must be happy, then again maybe not.

> *(Horn gets out of the pool. A meteorite. Silence. The flame flashes. House lights. Sound of the fountain bubbling. Water draining. Water drains.)*

Curtain

RUMINATIONS

CHARACTERS

KAROL: woman thirties.

HAROLD: man same age.

FARMER: man

SET: Yard off of a house. The house is not visible. Downstage a wooden fence from left to right. There is a 2 metre opening in the middle of the fence.

MUSIC: Sound indications in the text are abstracted by music: bells, thunder, cows, are mentioned in the dialogue and heard musically.

(Church bell rings in the distance. Harold enters. Karol enters.)

HAROLD: It is strange that church bells are ringing at this time of night.

KAROL: Yes.

HAROLD: If I were in the belfry I'd be ringing them softly.

KAROL: It's the timer in the bell tower, it's broken. So they ring at this time of night. Then it wakes me up.

HAROLD: If you had been sleeping I'd have woken you up and asked you how you had slept.

KAROL: I had only just got to sleep.

HAROLD: You were probably starting to dream?

KAROL: Yes.

HAROLD: I was going to ask you what your dreams were?

KAROL: I'd have to try and remember them.

(Bells stop ringing.)

HAROLD: So I had a strange dream this morning. I had woken up because my nose was bleeding. I might have bled to death if I had not woken up. What happened was that I had rolled over in bed to see who was there and I must have rolled over on my nose. Then I went back to sleep and dreamt that you were next to me. I wasn't sure if I was awake or asleep and I woke up and went back to sleep several times, this went on for quite a while until I got tired of getting up and going back to sleep, so

I got up to have breakfast. It was late and by that time I was quite hungry.

(Music, thunder.)

Then it's a pleasant night.

KAROL: It is.

HAROLD: Peaceful.

KAROL: Except for the thunder.

HAROLD: The storm is getting louder.

KAROL: Yes.

HAROLD: I was wondering if it'd thunder tonight.

KAROL: It has been.

HAROLD: I was afraid I'd be caught in the rain on my way here. And if I were to stay, in case it rains.

KAROL: You wouldn't want to. I might not be staying here myself.

(Music, thunder.)

HAROLD: And if we'd rather go somewhere else, we could, we could go away somewhere, take a trip across the ocean. To a place where the surroundings would be interesting enough to inspire us.

KAROL: Where to?

HAROLD: Where there is an ocean and a ship for us to sail away on to the end of the world. Then we could be washed overboard into the sea, if a storm were to come along.

KAROL: The sea would be rough.

HAROLD: A fury, but we wouldn't have to worry.

KAROL: But I would worry?

HAROLD: There wouldn't be any reason to, as long as we are only imagining it.

KAROL: But I worry.

HAROLD: Then I have some reservations, too.

KAROL: I can't help myself.

HAROLD: In a nearby country inn. Then the road for us to take is open to adventurers who are on their way. It's an old road for old people to walk down, who are hoping to become young again, thinking it would be nice to go away somewhere and start over. It might be called the Old Road, that Dusty Old Road.

KAROL: Ah.

HAROLD: Then there is Memory Lane. You know, I used to run down it and never look back. Memory Lane, a lot of things happened there. Most we've forgotten, and I have some souvenirs from my days on Memory Lane.

> (*He takes out a baby rattle from a pocket. The rattle has a pink ball on the end of its stem.*)

This is a baby's rattle. From my days on Memory Lane.

> (*He rubs the rattle provocatively on her stomach and down. He shakes the rattle.*)

Thunder. Invite me in. Or we could be struck by lightening.

(*Rattles.*)

KAROL: No.

HAROLD: If only nothing happened to discourage us.

KAROL: And then?

(*The bell to the front gate of the house is rung offstage; a messenger arrives offstage.*)

HAROLD: Something is happening. We are being interrupted, probably not for the better.

KAROL: Who is it?

(*He returns the rattle to his pocket.*)

HAROLD: I've been followed, because wherever I go I am always being followed.

(*He moves to exit.*)

Yes, I know who it is.

KAROL: If it's for you I'll let you get it.

(*Bell rings.*)

HAROLD: Listen to him.

KAROL: Well?

(*Male voice hums offstage.*)

HAROLD (*to man offstage*): I see you are there.

(*Humming stops.*)

It will be to deliver a birthday card from my mother to remind me that she is missed. (*Harold exits. Offstage.*) You found me.

(Harold enters with two envelopes, opening one.)

HAROLD: It says.

(Reads the letter.)

She's dying, is what it says.

(He drops the letter. Opens the other envelope. Reads it.)

She's dead. She has died.

KAROL: When?

HAROLD: This morning apparently, and I am finding out about it now.

(beat)

KAROL: How?

(He drops the letter.)

HAROLD: I imagine. We will have to go back for the funeral.

KAROL: You'd be expected to.

HAROLD: I would be.

KAROL: To make the arrangements.

HAROLD: Yes, I don't know.

KAROL: That is usually how it's done.

HAROLD: I would be too upset.

KAROL: It's the family's obligation.

HAROLD: I won't be of much use.

KAROL: No, you might not be.

HAROLD: It seems like I don't care.

KAROL: It's the shock at first. You don't believe it.

> *(beat)*

HAROLD: We will have to go to the funeral, in a day or two. That will give me some time to think about it. I am thirsty.

KAROL: I can get you something.

HAROLD: To drink.

KAROL: Water.

HAROLD: Please.

KAROL: I'll get it.

HAROLD: Please.

> *(Karol instantly hands Harold an enormous glass of water. Eight inches in diameter. A foot from top to bottom.)*

Thank you.

KAROL: Here.

HAROLD: It looks empty.

KAROL: What?

HAROLD: The glass.

KAROL: If I filled it up you wouldn't be able to lift it.

HAROLD: It's a very large glass.

KAROL: I have it for visitors.

HAROLD: Why such a big glass?

KAROL: It's a conversation piece.

(He drinks.)

HAROLD: The water is warm. There's no cold water?

KAROL: No.

HAROLD: No ice?

KAROL: It's melted.

(He drinks.)

HAROLD: Ah.

KAROL: It's enough?

HAROLD: Ah.

KAROL: I can get more.

(Drinks.)

Finished?

HAROLD *(mouth still in the glass drinking)*: Almost.

KAROL: Give me the glass when you are done.

(Cows mooing, maybe a cello playing.)

HAROLD: Cows. There are cows out there?

KAROL: There are. They come over here at night, since the fields were opened. Sometimes they roam at this time of night.

HAROLD: They're moseying along.

KAROL: Yes.

(Cow moos. He drinks from the glass.)

HAROLD: The glass is empty.

(He talks into the empty glass. Voice echoes in the glass.)

HAROLD: Empty. I feel empty too.

(He hums in the glass. Cows moo.)

KAROL: I'll take it.

(She takes the glass from him.)

HAROLD: These cows, at a time like this, but of course life must go on. *(pause)* And to the cow it is as if the frailty of life were meaningless, my God.

(She puts the glass down.)

It must be nice to be a part of a large group like that, and know you belong.

KAROL: "The sense of one's individuality is lost in the herd, and the whole is greater than the sum of its parts."

HAROLD: What? What's that?

KAROL: That was said by someone.

HAROLD: Was it?

KAROL: I believe so.

HAROLD: A quote.

KAROL: Yes.

HAROLD: What did they mean?

KAROL: Taken out of context it doesn't make sense.

HAROLD: What was the context?

KAROL: I don't remember.

HAROLD: You remember the quote.

KAROL: I may not remember it correctly.

HAROLD: Say it again.

KAROL: Ah...

HAROLD: It makes some sense.

KAROL: "The sense of one's individuality is lost in the herd, and the whole is greater than the sum of its parts."

HAROLD: Yet maybe it doesn't make any sense!

KAROL: It might or it might not.

HAROLD: The sum? What sum?

KAROL: You're the mathematician.

HAROLD: Yes, but I work with real numbers and symbols that represent numbers. Then you know I would have liked to have gone on into higher mathematics into abstract harmonic analysis where the calculations are minuscule and inconceivably small or impossibly large and there is not a reason for looking for an answer.

   (Mooing.)

Look, there are times when I don't pay attention to what is happening around me. I look around and I don't notice much, except myself and those I come in contact with.

   (A light narrows on him.)

Then it is uncommon to exceed all the expectations of others on all accounts. Then I possess talent, know-how, expertise. I have pursued unexplored avenues and future innovation. I am a forward-looking genius. The analogy I like to use is that I am an omnipotent astronomer, seen by followers to be the only visible star on a cloudy night. I am what those beneath me, the insignificant would like to be, less insignificant, whereas I am more so. They are the clouds and I shine through them showing them to be nothing more than dark shadows in my light, and on I shine for those in the dark. I am the light by which others can see. Then my outstanding accomplishments have been significantly important enough. I have been admired, worshipped, praised by peers, and certain individuals, subordinates, underlings, my apostles revere me as a saviour, their only guiding light. I shouldn't have to thank them... Then my real accomplishments, my notable achievements are those of a man of our time. And I'd like to be of my own time. To stand out as an example of what it is that we are living in this age, while at the same time maintaining a kind of de-tachment to it all.

(Spot widens.)

KAROL: You might become too detached.

HAROLD: A little.

KAROL: Then impotent.

HAROLD: I'd kill myself then.

(Mooing.)

What are they doing?

KAROL: They see a greener pasture.

HAROLD: But really I'd have preferred not to have been envied.

KAROL: Oh well.

HAROLD: Then sometimes I envied myself. I was jealous of my own success. How is it possible to do so well from so little effort? Yes, I can boast of my humility and not be hypocritcal.

(Karol quietly laughs.)

But then I can remember being made a fool of, and what was worse was that I was not willing to admit it even when being laughed at.

(He picks up one of the letters.)

I'll keep the letter.

(He picks up the other letter. Reads it.)

It doesn't mention anything about the arrangements.

(He gives her the letter.)

I wish it was over.

KAROL: Soon it will be.

HAROLD: Not soon enough. Nothing happens soon enough, or either it happens too quickly.

(She gives him back the letter.)

I will pay my tributes and cry. If I can or I'll keep my emotions to myself.

(Lights begin fading.)

HAROLD: So my emotions are not what they should be, and when I'm laughing I should be crying and when I'm sad I should be happy. But I look at you and I get my hopes up and yours? Could I get your hopes up? Could I?

KAROL: Oh.

HAROLD: There is hope. Let's lie if there isn't. Or would we be better off indifferent?

KAROL: No.

HAROLD: If we could be indifferent for a few moments and stop living and die, then come back to life after a few missing heartbeats, so long enough to come back rested after a few moments on the other side. Rested, at peace, finally at peace. What do you think?

KAROL: For a few seconds, why not?

HAROLD: I don't mean too long.

KAROL: No.

HAROLD: For a few seconds.

KAROL: Shh.

(Mooing. Gust of wind, a billow of white noise.)

The night in the fields has taken the wind out of the air. I remember that from a poem. The cows are looking at the moon curiously. In some lands the cow is seen as a holy animal. And they are moonstruck. They are gazing at the moon. Grazing at the moon.

HAROLD: It's dark.

(Karol moves to the opening in the railing.)

KAROL: They are as curious as we are. Come on.

HAROLD: It's dark.

KAROL: Come.

HAROLD: Where?

KAROL: Follow me.

(Harold and Karol step outside the railing, as the they do so the lights fade almost to black. They are backlit. Shadows.)

The dew is up, our shoes will get wet.

HAROLD: They are wet already. But I am afraid of running into a tree.

KAROL: No, there are no trees in this field. They were chopped down. The stumps were pulled out.

HAROLD: When was that?

KAROL: Some long time ago.

HAROLD: And there will never be any replanting?

KAROL: No.

HAROLD: Do you think that someone somewhere would be interested to know that I'm thinking about what the ruler of the world would be thinking about? Imagine. But it doesn't matter. Because of course there are not any more great rulers. Maybe there never were. So if we were God? If I were? If you were? Both of us. What would we be thinking?

KAROL: Me?

HAROLD: As if by a miracle to be thinking what He

was thinking.

(They step back into the yard, and as they return the lights fade up.)

HAROLD: Suppose.

KAROL: As if what.

(Lights dim.)

HAROLD: Then after having slept in your arms, on a cold winter night when you were so warm.

KAROL: On a hot summer's night cooling off next to your corpse.

HAROLD: If we dream of a wedding there will be a funeral soon. But if we dream of a funeral will there be a wedding soon? One final dream.

(The following unit is a shared dream. A cello modulates under the voices, continuing until the end of the unit. The text should be delivered as a quick spoken song.)

I was watching you from a hole in the ground.

(The unison parts are spoken with the underlined words of unison 1 matching the double underline of unison 2.)

KAROL *(solo)*: You are watching me from a hole —

HAROLD *(unison 1)*: You were in a field, there was a herd of cows following you. At the other end of the field a barn was on fire —

KAROL *(unison 2)*: — in the ground, your family grave. A herd of cows is following me through a field towards a barn that is on <u>fire</u>.

HAROLD *(solo)*: You walked towards the barn —

KAROL *(unison 1)*: The cows run... the cows run... <u>stampeding</u> into the <u>flames</u>.

HAROLD *(unison 2)*: The cows were following you. When you got to the door. The animals began to <u>stampede</u>, they ran into the <u>flames</u>.

HAROLD *(solo)*: Their moos were heard for miles —

KAROL *(unison 1)*: <u>The next day</u> you see me addressing a group of <u>people defending the rights of animals.</u> <u>People are applauding me</u> —

HAROLD *(unison 2)*: <u>— the next day</u> — you were up on a platform talking to a group of <u>people, defending the rights of animals. People were applauding you</u> —

KAROL *(unison 1)*: — <u>Of course, no one knew of my previous day's cruelty, of the cows that were still smoldering in the barn as I spoke.</u>

HAROLD *(unison 2)*: — <u>Of course, no one knew of your previous day's cruelty, of the cows that were still smoldering in the barn as you smoked</u>.

KAROL: Smoked?

HAROLD: Spoke.

> *(Lights come up.)*

KAROL: What was that?

HAROLD: You were speaking in tongues. It was only a dream?

KAROL: It's madness, Harold, madness.

HAROLD: It is madness, and we've been crazy before.

KAROL: Which is worrisome.

HAROLD: But do you know what I aspire to, is to be everything that is divine in you. To be thinking what God was thinking about, to be thinking about you.

KAROL: No, don't do that.

HAROLD: I would like to, to aspire to that.

KAROL: Please.

HAROLD: With my heart. My soul.

KAROL: Sh.

HAROLD: My aspirations are yours.

KAROL: God no.

HAROLD: It may be possible for us to get married—

KAROL: Oh.

HAROLD: So that we can make demands on each other and never feel guilty. After the funeral we can get married. And whatever our plans are — I'd leave it up to you. I'd be happy knowing a decision was made by someone. By you?

KAROL: By me.

HAROLD: Then I could agree with you after having made the original suggestion. Don't think about it. We do too much of that.

KAROL: But financially, what is your situation now? Has it improved maybe?

HAROLD: Yes, I've done well enough. I think I even have more than I need really. And there will be money passed on, money that the family would have wanted to have given away to the poor, and we can give it away, or maybe keep some of it, give the rest to charity. We could put our efforts into giving money away instead of taking it for ourselves. Many of the problems of the world would be solved if more people did so.

KAROL: What?

HAROLD: Why not be happy with what we need and give away what is unnecessary? We could be poor, poor and in love.

KAROL: What are you saying?

HAROLD: I should have other uses for adding things up than just for the sake of counting money.

KAROL: Have I heard you correctly? What are you saying actually? No, you just don't want to have to work too hard, and you don't have any idea of what working to exhaustion does to one, what happens to a person. And Harold, it's not for who, it's not for whom. No, for God's sake, and there are those who think they might have it so easy who are supposedly independent, then that makes a difference! No, it does not. I'll give an example? For example, a farmer. The real independent farmer, he has his business, but it is all the same for a person who thinks he is independent. Because there's a good possibility that things can go wrong from the beginning, and for a farmer, as an example, the weather won't co-operate, or there will be a drought or it will hail or the markets collapse.

HAROLD: I can understand that.

KAROL: You don't understand.

HAROLD: I don't know much about farmers.

KAROL: What do you know about farmers? I grew up with them.

HAROLD: Nothing.

KAROL: Ask me then. I grew up with these people!

HAROLD: What would I ask?

KAROL: What is a farmer? Ask me what is a farmer? And why do they work themselves to death? What makes him work?! Why do they do it? Because like so many they're convinced that things will improve if they work hard enough. And I grew up with farmers! My family were farmers. And to a farmer; the family, the family is important. And the farmer and his family, what are they like, standing in shit with their illiterate children. Proud of their stupidity and ignorance, hating themselves and their friends. I was surrounded by people who hated themselves and everyone around them. They despised each other. The neighbours. People in their own families. And it's not only the farmers, but their friends, and the friends of farmer's friends, and all their ancestors and their children, and their children's children, and all their friends, and just about anyone who is alive or who has ever lived, because they were all of the sudden poor. Don't ask me to be poor. I will never be poor. Never!

HAROLD: Yes, I suppose I've wanted to forget what it was like to be poor.

KAROL: I'll never forget!

HAROLD: No, I haven't forgotten either. I'd like to.

KAROL: Let's not kid each other.

HAROLD: Well, I wasn't serious.

(Pause. They laugh.)

KAROL: It's late.

(pause)

HAROLD: But what are we arguing about? *(beat)* I would hope that things would change without us knowing it. Suddenly out of the blue.

KAROL: There were trees here but they were taken down for pasture... by farmers.

HAROLD: And when looking at the past again.

(He rattles the rattle in his pocket. Takes out the rattle. Again light narrows on him.)

The past.

(Rattles.)

Then I would like to believe that there is nothing we don't really understand, though there are subjects that we always have doubts about, I don't know. But whatever doubts we may have are only because of what we are unaware of, so why worry? I don't.

(Rattles.)

I don't know maybe it isn't healthy to live in one's fantasies. But what else is there?

(beat)

KAROL: Then we will get married.

HAROLD: Day after tomorrow.

KAROL: We will be in mourning.

HAROLD: Some time after the funeral.

KAROL: It is soon. You wouldn't want to be sad.

HAROLD: It will make me feel better.

KAROL: Hm.

(*Church bells ring.*)

The church will be torn down soon and now the bells are ringing for the last time.

(*Music. It is the next day.*)

HAROLD: Funeral bells.

KAROL: And wedding bells.

(*The following unit is spoken quickly.*)

HAROLD: Are we ready for the married life?

KAROL: By now we should be.

HAROLD: We will have to go on a trip afterwards.

KAROL: Let it be endless.

HAROLD: Off to a new world.

KAROL: As long as it's better than the old one.

HAROLD: Let us make a promise that it will be.

KAROL: We wouldn't want to be too optimistic and risk being disappointed.

HAROLD: How shall we be married?

KAROL: By accident, a fatal one.

HAROLD: I would die for you.

KAROL: You might have to.

HAROLD: Ask me and I would.

KAROL: I shouldn't have to ask.

HAROLD: Let's make it a love suicide.

KAROL: The only way to go.

HAROLD: I love you.

KAROL: Till death.

HAROLD: Whenever that may be.

KAROL: Soon.

HAROLD: Any time is fine with me.

KAROL: Me too.

HAROLD: Now?

KAROL: Why hurry?

HAROLD: We might not have much time left.

KAROL: We don't.

HAROLD: How much time is there ever really?

KAROL: Less and less.

HAROLD: Kill me.

KAROL: I'd like to.

HAROLD: I want to die, to forget that I had ever lived
   a horrible life.

KAROL *(beat)*: And now I love you.

HAROLD: We can die peacefully now.

KAROL: Yes, we can.

HAROLD: Hoping that we won't.

KAROL: Hoping against hope.

(*Church bells.*)

They are ringing for the last time.

(*They walk around circling.*)

HAROLD: Off we go west into the setting sun.

KAROL: By the time we got there, it would be rising in the east.

HAROLD: At least we would be headed in the right direction.

(*She sits on the floor between the two railings.*)

KAROL: Why not go to sleep now?

HAROLD: Wouldn't it be better to stay awake and never sleep.

KAROL: Not if you're tired.

(*She lies down.*)

HAROLD: I can remember being tired when I was younger. I thought I was getting older, but I was just tired, especially in the mornings and late at night.

(*Birds chirp.*)

Funny, a bird landed on the windowsill the other morning. It woke me up. It was a songbird. I slammed the window and accidentally killed it.

As it was dying it laid an egg. I had it for breakfast. Then you know how much I hate eggs and love birds. And it might be one of those variety of birds that mate for life. And when it's over then what do they do? When one bird is gone, what does the other bird do? What do we do?

KAROL: Separate.

HAROLD: I would have liked to have spent eternity with you.

KAROL: No, the distance between us is eternal.

HAROLD: My death bed will be lonely without you.

KAROL: A death bed is always lonely.

> (*Lights fade.*)

Epilogue

HAROLD: It shouldn't be. Unless we were to go together.

KAROL: We will.

HAROLD: What those who love each other would always hope for.

KAROL: Yes.

> (*pause*)

HAROLD: I have a gun. (*beat*) I've had it with me as I thought I might need it, since I was a child, from my days on Memory Lane.

> (*He gives her a small toy handgun that was in his pocket.*)

KAROL: I too am armed.

(*She takes out a handgun. Hands it to him.*)

I got it when I heard you out here, I didn't know it was you.

(*She points the gun in his direction.*)

HAROLD: Would you?

KAROL: No.

HAROLD: There is no reason to be afraid now.

KAROL: No.

(*He points his gun at her. They are aiming the guns at one another.*)

We wouldn't ever be tempted?

HAROLD: It's a toy, I meant to get a real one, but I'm not as romantic as I'd like to be.

KAROL: It's a toy.

HAROLD: This is not a toy. I can't tell the difference.

(*Thunder in the distance. They set the guns down on the railing.*)

KAROL: Somewhere there are millions shooting. They are shooting and will go on shooting and will continue to do so for some time to come.

(*Music interlude. Lights come up bright for the first time. It is daytime.*)

HAROLD: That happened?

KAROL: Yes.

HAROLD: The night before we were married.

> *(Enter farmer carrying a pitchfork with a bundle of hay on the fork. He has a cowbell around his neck. He is ringing the bell.)*

FARMER: Excuse me. Excuse me. Hello.

HAROLD: Hello.

FARMER: Have you seen one of my animals?

HAROLD: No.

FARMER: One on the run.

KAROL: No.

HAROLD: Haven't seen one.

KAROL: Neither have I.

FARMER: No, no one ever sees them. Fine. All right. It's not a problem. Christ. God-damn it. Fucking people. And now it's going to rain. Damn it. Fuck.

> *(Farmer exits ringing cowbell.)*

HAROLD: It will have been years since then.

KAROL: Yes it has.

HAROLD: A farmer came along earlier looking for a cow.

KAROL: Yes, I was there. I was standing where I am. I haven't moved.

HAROLD: I guess you were.

KAROL: Do you think he found her?

HAROLD: They usually do, don't they?

KAROL: He ought to have told us if he had.

HAROLD: I've been wondering if he had.

KAROL: We don't really have much to say to one another any more.

HAROLD: I can't think of anything.

KAROL: Neither can I.

HAROLD: And I once said that we'd die of boredom.

KAROL: It won't be because of the excitement.

HAROLD: No.

KAROL: It won't.

HAROLD: That's what I said.

KAROL: It won't be for the excitement.

HAROLD: You said the same thing after me.

KAROL: We had left.

HAROLD: By then.

KAROL: We were gone.

HAROLD: So then, for some time, by my calculations, it would would appear as if eternity was well on its way, and it is.

> *(Karol and Harold exit backing away slowly in opposite directions, looking at each other. Lights fade. Enter farmer with pitchfork ringing cow bell. He looks in either direction. Cello plays. Farmer exits. Blackout. Silence.)*

Curtain

www.ingramcontent.com/pod-product-compliance
Lightning Source LLC
Chambersburg PA
CBHW051005050726
47592CB00007B/2716